Copyright ©

All rights reserved. This book or any portion thereof may not be reproduced or used in any manner whatsoever without the express written permission of the publisher except for the use of brief quotations in a book review

WELCOME TO "TRY NOT TO LAUGH CHALLENGE"

RULES OF THE GAME

- ⚡ 2player play this game so you batter grab a friend or a family member, Determine who will be player 1 and player 2

- ⚡ one at a time, players reading the jokes aloud to each other, check the box for each joke you get a laugh of it, there are guides in pages to each player turn

- ⚡ when the players completed all the jokes in the round, mark all the points down in the score rounds 10 page, there is a total of

- ⚡ Play as many rounds as you like once you reach the last round, write down the total score of all rounds in the page that customize for it to determine who is " try not to laugh " champion

Player1

Now is Time To Play

Player2

Round 1

Player 1

What time is it when the clock strikes 13 ?

Time to get a new clock

◯ LAUGH

How does a cucumber become a pickle?

It goes through a jarring experience

◯ LAUGH

What did one toilet say to the other?

You look a bit flushed

◯ LAUGH

What do you think of that new diner on the moon?

Food was good, but there really wasn't much atmosphere

◯ LAUGH

Player 1

What does a cloud wear under his raincoat?

⬡ LAUGH

Thunderwear

Two pickles fell out of a jar onto the floor. What did one say to the other?

⬡ LAUGH

Dill with it

What do you call a boomerang that won't come back?

⬡ LAUGH

A stick

Why did the dinosaur cross the road?

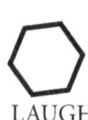

⬡ LAUGH

Because the chicken wasn't born yet

Player 2

What did the cat say when he fell off the table? ⬡ LAUGH

"Me-ow."

What do you get when you cross a ball and a cat? ⬡ LAUGH

A fur ball

Why didn't the skeleton go to school? ⬡ LAUGH

His heart wasn't in it

How does a vampire start a letter? ⬡ LAUGH

Tomb it may concern…

Player 2

What's a cat's favorite magazine?

A cat-alogue

What cat likes living in water?

An octo-puss

What is a monster's favorite dessert?

I scream

What monster plays tricks on Halloween?

Prank-enstein

Player 1

____ /8

vs

____ /8

Player 2

ROUND CHAMPION

_____

Round 2

Player 1

Why can't Elsa from Frozen have a balloon?

⬡ LAUGH

Because she will "let it go, let it go".

What musical instrument is found in the bathroom?

⬡ LAUGH

A tuba toothpaste.

Why did the kid bring a ladder to school?

⬡ LAUGH

Because she wanted to go to high school

What do you call a dog magician?

⬡ LAUGH

A labracadabrador

Player 1

Where would you find an elephant?

○ LAUGH

The same place you lost her

How do you get a squirrel to like you?

○ LAUGH

Act like a nut

What building in your town has the most stories?

○ LAUGH

The public library

What's worse than finding a worm in your apple?

○ LAUGH

Finding half a worm

Player 2

What kind of music do mummies love?

◯ LAUGH

Wrap music

What fruit do scarecrows love the most?

◯ LAUGH

Straw-berries

What does a witch use to do her hair?

◯ LAUGH

Scarespray

What room does a ghost not need?

◯ LAUGH

A living room

Player 2

What kind of dog does Dracula have?

○ LAUGH

A blood hound

What is a ghost's nose full of?

○ LAUGH

Boo-gers

What do birds say on Halloween?

○ LAUGH

Trick or tweet

How do you fix a cracked pumpkin?

○ LAUGH

A pumpkin patch

Player 1

____ /8

vs

____ /8

Player 2

ROUND CHAMPION

____

Round 3

Player 1

What is a computer's favorite snack?

Computer chips

◯ LAUGH

What did one volcano say to the other?

I lava you

◯ LAUGH

How do we know that the ocean is friendly?

It waves

◯ LAUGH

What is a tornado's favorite game to play?

Twister

◯ LAUGH

Player 1

How does the moon cut his hair?

○ LAUGH

Eclipse it

How do you talk to a giant?

○ LAUGH

Use big words

What animal is always at a baseball game?

○ LAUGH

A bat

What falls in winter but never gets hurt?

○ LAUGH

Snow

Player 2

When is it bad luck to be followed by a black cat?
◯ LAUGH

When you're a mouse

What do you call two witches living together?
◯ LAUGH

Broommates

What happens when a vampire goes in the snow?
◯ LAUGH

Frost bite

Why did the zombie skip school?
◯ LAUGH

He was feeling rotten

Player 2

What is a vampire's favorite fruit?

◯ LAUGH

A blood orange

What instrument does a skeleton play?

◯ LAUGH

The trom-bone

Where do baby ghosts go during the day?

◯ LAUGH

Day-scare centers

Why didn't the skeleton go to the dance?

◯ LAUGH

Because he had no body to go with

Player 1

_ _ _ _ _ /8

vs

_ _ _ _ _ /8

Player 2

ROUND CHAMPION

_ _ _ _ _ _ _

Round 4

Player 1

What did the Dalmatian say after lunch?

That hit the spot

⬡ LAUGH

Why did the kid cross the playground?

To get to the other slide

⬡ LAUGH

What do you call a droid that takes the long way around?

R2 detour

⬡ LAUGH

Why did the cookie go to the hospital?

Because he felt crummy

⬡ LAUGH

Player 1

Why was the baby strawberry crying?

Because her mom and dad were in a jam

⬡ LAUGH

What did the little corn say to the mama corn?

Where is pop corn?

⬡ LAUGH

How do you make a lemon drop?

Just let it fall

⬡ LAUGH

What did the limestone say to the geologist?

Don't take me for granite

⬡ LAUGH

Player 2

What candy do you eat on the playground?

⬡ LAUGH

Recess pieces

What's a witch's favorite subject in school?

⬡ LAUGH

Spelling

What's big, scary and has three wheels?

⬡ LAUGH

A monster on a tricycle

Why don't vampires have more friends?

⬡ LAUGH

Because they are a pain in the neck

Player 2

What position does a ghost play in hockey?

○ LAUGH

Ghoulie

What do you call a witch who goes to the beach?

○ LAUGH

A sand-witch

What do you give a vampire when he's sick?

○ LAUGH

Coffin drops

What kinds of pants do ghosts wear?

○ LAUGH

Boo-jeans

Player 1

_ _ _ _ /8

vs

_ _ _ _ /8

Player 2

ROUND CHAMPION

_ _ _ _ _ _ _

Round 5

Player 1

Why does a seagull fly over the sea?

○ LAUGH

Because if it flew over the bay, it would be a baygull

What kind of water can't freeze?

○ LAUGH

Hot water

What kind of tree fits in your hand?

○ LAUGH

A palm tree

What do you call a dinosaur that is sleeping?

○ LAUGH

A dino-snore

Player 1

What is fast, loud and crunchy?

◯ LAUGH

A rocket chip

Why did the teddy bear say no to dessert?

◯ LAUGH

Because she was stuffed

What has ears but cannot hear?

◯ LAUGH

A cornfield

What did the left eye say to the right eye?

◯ LAUGH

Between us, something smells

Player 2

Who isn't hungry at Thanksgiving?

○ LAUGH

The turkey—he's already stuffed

Can a turkey jump higher than Mount Everest?

○ LAUGH

Yes, because a building can't jump at all

Which side of the turkey has the most feathers?

○ LAUGH

The outside

What always comes at the end of Thanksgiving?

○ LAUGH

The letter g

Player 2

What's the key to a great Thanksgiving dinner?
⬡ LAUGH

The tur-key

Where does Christmas come before Thanksgiving?
⬡ LAUGH

In the dictionary

Why did pilgrims' pants always fall down?
⬡ LAUGH

Because they wore their belt buckle on their hat

What do turkeys and teddy bears have in common?
⬡ LAUGH

They both have stuffing

Player 1

_ _ _ _ /8

vs

_ _ _ _ /8

Player 2

ROUND CHAMPION

_ _ _ _ _

Round 6

Player 1

What did one plate say to the other plate?

Dinner is on me

○ LAUGH

Why did the student eat his homework?

Because the teacher told him it was a piece of cake

○ LAUGH

What is brown, hairy and wears sunglasses?

A coconut on vacation

○ LAUGH

What do you say to a rabbit on its birthday?

Hoppy Birthday

○ LAUGH

Player 1

Why do candles always go on the top of cakes?

LAUGH

Because it's hard to light them from the bottom

What do cakes and baseball teams have in common?

LAUGH

They both need a good batter

What goes up but never comes down?

LAUGH

Your age

What did the tiger say to her cub on his birthday?

LAUGH

It's roar birthday

Player 2

What key won't open any door?

○ LAUGH

A turkey

Why did the turkey cross the road?

○ LAUGH

It was the chicken's day off

Why did the chewing gum cross the road?

○ LAUGH

It was stuck on the turkey's foot

Why did the turkey cross the road twice?

○ LAUGH

To show he wasn't a chicken

Player 2

Why was the turkey the drummer in the band?

◯ LAUGH

Because he had drumsticks

What's the best thing to put into pumpkin pie?

◯ LAUGH

Your teeth

What's the best dance to do on Thanksgiving?

◯ LAUGH

The turkey trot

Why did the Pilgrims sail from England to America?

◯ LAUGH

Because they missed their plane

Player 1

_ _ _ _ /8

vs

_ _ _ _ /8

Player 2

ROUND CHAMPION

_ _ _ _ _ _ _ _

Round 7

Player 1

Why did the girl put her cake in the freezer?

◯ LAUGH

She wanted to ice it

Does a green candle burn longer than a pink one?

◯ LAUGH

No, they both burn shorter

Why did the little girl hit her birthday cake with a hammer?

◯ LAUGH

It was a pound cake

Why is the obtuse triangle always so frustrated?

◯ LAUGH

Because it's never right

Player 1

Why is six afraid of seven?

Because seven eight nine ◯ LAUGH

Why was the equal sign so humble?

Because he wasn't greater than or less than anyone else ◯ LAUGH

Why couldn't the pony sing a lullaby?

She was a little horse ◯ LAUGH

What was the first animal in space?

The cow that jumped over the moon ◯ LAUGH

Player 2

When the Pilgrims landed, where did they stand?

⬡ LAUGH

On their feet

Why did the police arrest the turkey?

⬡ LAUGH

They suspected it of fowl play

Why was the Easter Bunny so upset?

⬡ LAUGH

He was having a bad hare day

How did the soggy Easter Bunny dry himself?

⬡ LAUGH

With a hare dryer

Player 2

How does the Easter bunny stay in shape?

○ LAUGH

Lots of eggs-ercise

Why can't a rabbit's nose be 12 inches long?

○ LAUGH

Because then it would be a foot

How can you tell which rabbits are the oldest in a group?

○ LAUGH

Just look for the gray hares

What do you call a bunny who isn't smart?

○ LAUGH

A hare brain

Player 1

_ _ _ _ /8

vs

_ _ _ _ /8

Player 2

ROUND CHAMPION

_ _ _ _ _ _ _ _

Round 8

Player 1

Why don't elephants chew gum?

They do, just not in public ⬡ LAUGH

What did the banana say to the dog?

Bananas can't talk ⬡ LAUGH

What do you call guys who love math?

Algebros ⬡ LAUGH

Why was the fraction nervous about marrying the decimal?

Because he would have to convert ⬡ LAUGH

Player 1

How do you make an octopus laugh?

With ten-tickles

◯ LAUGH

What do you call a sleeping bull?

A bull-dozer

◯ LAUGH

How do you fit more pigs on a farm?

Build a sty-scraper

◯ LAUGH

What did the farmer call the cow that had no milk?

An udder failure

◯ LAUGH

Player 2

Who earns a living by driving their customers away?

○ LAUGH

A taxi driver!

What's big, scary, and has three wheels?

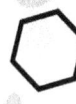

○ LAUGH

A monster riding a tricycle!

What's worse than raining cats and dogs?

○ LAUGH

Hailing taxis!

What happened when a red ship crashed into a blue ship?

○ LAUGH

The crew was marooned!

Player 2

What kind of plates do they use in space?

Flying saucers! LAUGH

When is a door not a door?

When it is ajar/a jar! LAUGH

Why did the woman run around her bed?

She wanted to catch up on her sleep! LAUGH

Why do fluorescent lights hum?

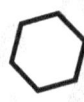

Because they forgot the words! LAUGH

Player 1

_ _ _ _ /8

vs

_ _ _ _ /8

Player 2

ROUND CHAMPION

Round 9

Player 1

What do you call a cow that won't give milk?

A milk dud

◯ LAUGH

Why do fish live in salt water?

Because pepper makes them sneeze

◯ LAUGH

What do you get from a pampered cow?

Spoiled milk

◯ LAUGH

Where do polar bears vote?

The North Poll

◯ LAUGH

Player 1

What sound do porcupines make when they kiss?

◯ LAUGH

Ouch!

Why did the snake cross the road?

◯ LAUGH

To get to the other ssside

Why are fish so smart?

◯ LAUGH

Because they live in schools

Why don't pirates shower before they walk the plank?

◯ LAUGH

Because they'll just wash up on shore later

Player 2

Why did the house go to the doctor?

Because it had a window pane/pain! ⬡ LAUGH

What did the quilt say to the bed?

⬡ LAUGH

I've got you covered!

What should you do if you find a dinosaur in your bed?

⬡ LAUGH

Find somewhere else to sleep!

How do you know if there's a dinosaur under your bed?

⬡ LAUGH

Your nose hits the ceiling!

Player 2

What goes up when the rain comes down?

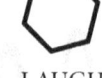

An umbrella! ⬡ LAUGH

Why do witches fly on brooms?

Because vacuum cleaners are too heavy! ⬡ LAUGH

How do you know if there's a dinosaur in your refrigerator?

Look for footprints in the pizza! ⬡ LAUGH

How do you warm up a room after it's been painted?

Give it a second coat! ⬡ LAUGH

Player 1

_ _ _ _ _ /8

vs

_ _ _ _ _ /8

Player 2

ROUND CHAMPION

Round 10

Player 1

What has 8 legs, 8 arms, and 8 eyes?

◯ LAUGH

∧ pirates

Why is pirating so addictive?

◯ LAUGH

They say once ye lose yer first hand, ye get hooked

How do pirates know that they are pirates?

◯ LAUGH

They think, therefore they arrr

What is a cat's favorite color?

◯ LAUGH

Purrr-ple

Player 1

What song does a cat like best?

Three Blind Mice ⬡ LAUGH

What kind of kitten works for the Red Cross?

A first-aid kit ⬡ LAUGH

Where did the school kittens go for their field trip?

To the mew-seum ⬡ LAUGH

Why are cats good at video games?

Because they have nine lives ⬡ LAUGH

Player 2

Where do snowmen love to dance?

At a snow ball ⬡ LAUGH

What did Jack Frost say to Frosty the Snowman?

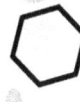

Have an ice day! ⬡ LAUGH

What does a gingerbread man put on his bed?

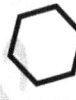

A cookie sheet ⬡ LAUGH

What do you have in December that you can't have in any other month?

The letter D ⬡ LAUGH

Player 2

What do you call a snowman temper tantrum?

A meltdown

○ LAUGH

What's the difference between a Christmas alphabet and the regular alphabet?

Have an ice day!

○ LAUGH

What did the icy road say to the truck?

Want to go for a spin?

○ LAUGH

What's a snowman's favorite drink?

Ice Tea

○ LAUGH

Player 1

_ _ _ _ _ /8

vs

_ _ _ _ _ /8

Player 2

ROUND CHAMPION

FINAL SCORE

P1 _____ /80

P2 _____ /80

THE " TRY NOT TO LAUGH CHALLENGE " CHAMPION IS

Thanks For Reading The Book We Hope is has been useful, if you like your book please we hope you can let us an Expressly reviewed.